WITHDRAWN
UTSA LIBRARIES

Our Lives Are Rivers

University of Central Florida Contemporary Poetry Series

Florida A&M University, Tallahassee
Florida Atlantic University, Boca Raton
Florida Gulf Coast University, Ft. Myers
Florida International University, Miami
Florida State University, Tallahassee
University of Central Florida, Orlando
University of Florida, Gainesville
University of North Florida, Jacksonville
University of South Florida, Tampa
University of West Florida, Pensacola

University Press of Florida
Gainesville
Tallahassee
Tampa
Boca Raton
Pensacola
Orlando
Miami
Jacksonville
Ft. Myers

Our Lives Are Rivers

Mark Smith-Soto

Copyright 2003 by Mark Smith-Soto
Printed in the United States of America on acid-free paper
All rights reserved

08 07 06 05 04 03 c 6 5 4 3 2 1
08 07 06 05 04 03 p 6 5 4 3 2 1

Library of Congress Cataloging-in-Publication Data
Smith-Soto, Mark I. (Mark Israel), 1948–
Our lives are rivers / Mark Smith-Soto.
p. cm. — (University of Central Florida contemporary poetry
series)
ISBN 0-8130-2634-2 (acid-free paper) —ISBN 0-8130-2635-0
(pbk.: acid-free paper)
1. Costa Rican Americans--Poetry. I Title. II. Contemporary
poetry series (Orlando, Fla.)
PS3619.M63O94 2003
811'.54--dc21   2003040240
Paperback cover and title page: *Inocencia,*
pastel drawing by Beth Adamour

The University Press of Florida is the scholarly publishing
agency for the State University System of Florida, comprising
Florida A&M University, Florida Atlantic University, Florida
Gulf Coast University, Florida International University, Florida
State University, University of Central Florida, University of
Florida, University of North Florida, University of South Florida,
and University of West Florida.

University Press of Florida
15 Northwest 15th Street
Gainesville, FL 32611-2079
http://www.upf.com

Para Beth,
ayer, hoy y siempre . . .
y para Anita, Alan y David

Pues si vemos lo presente
cómo en un punto se es ido
  y acabado,
si juzgamos sabiamente,
daremos lo non venido
  por pasado.

—Jorge Manrique

Contents

Acknowledgments

Several of the poems included in this collection first appeared in *Green Mango Collage,* winner of the 2000 North Carolina Writers' Network's Persephone Chapbook Publication Prize; and in *Shafts,* winner of the 2002 Randall Jarrell/Harperprints Poetry Chapbook Competition. "Isabel Soto Borbón" and "Tulia Soto de Smith," together with an early draft of "Aunt Aída Born Again," appeared under the title "Three Sisters" as a finalist for *Nimrod*'s 1986 Pablo Neruda Prize for Poetry. "First Movement" won *Chiron Review*'s 2000 Poetry Prize Competition.

Americas Review: "What I Mean," "Latino Born on the Brooklyn Bridge"; *Blue Pitcher:* "Before We Knew"; *Callaloo* (Johns Hopkins University Press): "Claudia and Love," "Witness"; *Carolina Quarterly:* "Easter Wings"; *Chattahoochee Review:* "Why I Am Afraid of Physical Harm"; *Chiron Review:* "First Movement"; *The Kenyon Review:* "Tomorrow, Yesterday"; *Nebraska Review:* "First Communion"; *Nimrod:* "Isabel Soto Borbón," "Tulia Soto de Smith"; *North Carolina Literary Review:* "After Another Death"; *Pleiades:* "Aunt Aída Born Again"; *Plum Review:* "Latino"; *Poetry East:* "The Parting"; *Potomac Review:* "Timex"; *Quarterly West:* "Café of Mirrors"; *Word and Witness: One Hundred Years of North Carolina Poetry:* "Bubble."

Ayer . . .

Tomorrow, Yesterday

Back when the future was firmly in its place
before Merrilee died and before Phoebe
her cat died, before my Uncle Marschall
died and before my mother, but after

my father died and my grandmothers and
my grandfather that I walked with in Alajuela
who loosened his belt and whistled playing
solitaire, after hateful Joaquín died but

before complicated much-missed Isabel
and long before Aída with her laughing
mean face and bony fingers, in the time
of Beth and Juanito and Johnny and sun

and wind caught in a bottle, and the fig tree
loaded hard and green against the side
of the house, and the mornings loaded
with the hunger of birds and the world loaded,

before Nureyev and Rock Hudson but after
Marilyn, back when the future was firmly
in its place and hangovers were worth it
and sex glittered in the air and shone

in our sinuses and to sneeze was to come
in a small way because we were going
to eat Camembert in the shadow of Chartres
and we were going to eat roast pork in Chinchón

and we were going to walk under the red
Alicante moon, holding hands, how innocent,
under the aged-Gouda moon, we were going
all the way, when the future was in its place

instead of where it's slinking now, hangdog,
dog-eared, smelling of days lost in some hole
never to be dug up again, the lovely hunger gone,
the figs, the long sweet breath of tomorrow.

Why I Am Afraid of Physical Harm

When I was a kid my little brother shot me
with an arrow and I saw it coming forever
like when a mirror is going to break it falls so slow

and then Chevo got a machete cut above the eye
and we saw him cry like a wild dog and maybe
that's why I am afraid of physical harm,

everybody is, I know, but when I was five
under the bed I gobbled the St. Joseph aspirin
and doctors forced a mile of water down my throat,

and always mother heaving with her black tides of
    asthma
and who could forget Zulema's stories of the boy
cleaning his gun who shot his beautiful sister who
    died,

and the boy who picked up a red, black, and yellow
    stick
that bit him and he died, and that other boy who kept
swallowing his gum into a great big ball in his belly so

he died, and the thin men smiling on street corners
who boil lost children into balls of blue soap,
and the wind in your face that makes you cross-eyed
    forever?

Isabel Soto Borbón

My fat Aunt Isabel,
big body bulging
in the neighbor's old tuxedo
and a neatly drawn mustache,
toddled through the room
to make us laugh—
how pigeon-toed she danced!
how her clever (blue,
green, strange and beautiful)
eyes rolled!
She was so heavy
the day parted where she passed,
and we stepped quick
and happy behind her,
snapping our fingers
like castanets.
She could be mean,
her pinches were something,
and her cry of "*Confiteros*!
I'll show you," meant fly
or be shown.
But who cared? She appeared
and boredom scurried
to its hole, my mother's asthma
was a thing of the past,
and even our father
laughed once—yes,
that was the day she discovered
Bill Haley and the Comets,
the latest spin from the pagan
dance-mad USA,
she sailed into our house
and blew the windows away.
It was in that country

of our childhood, in that house
by a bridge still stomped
by oxen, in that long living room
brightened by Zulema the maid,
that Bill Haley tore
out of black plastic,
and how, how
fat Aunt Isabel rocked!
With the music banging
a wonderful soreness
in the air, how we rocked
with her!
She was the ball
down the long hall,
we were the pins
bounced off the wall,
she was Jupiter,
we were her moons,
she was the band,
we were the music that she made.
Was it from her we learned
life could be had?
It *was* from her we learned
life could be had.
And now (which is why
I write these words that can't
begin to remember her)
in a small hospital
of a small country,
fatter than ever with dropsy
and gift candy from friends,
my Aunt Isabel
dies in a bed,
and how I hope it's not

a narrow bed,
and how I hope her nurses
are not little nurses,
and how I hope from so many
miles and years away
that the sheets that hold her
may stretch over her
huge and gentle,
free as sails.

Tulia Soto de Smith

Dear Tulia,
squat parrot eyeing me
from your absolute perch
in the purgatory
of your dreams—
will you forgive me
in the end?
Will I forgive you?
I see you
preening there,
breathing in the amnesia
of self-righteousness,
and wonder:
how are you doing
this fine March fifth?
Does your liver burn?
How's that old humped back?
How are those eyes
that frightened cats?
How's that ugly-fruit heart?
Seventy years
have made their nest in you,
and still I know right now you are
out for a stroll
under the Costa Rican palms,
swinging your purse
like a ten-year-old,
and no one looking at you
would guess the fairy-tale princess
behind the washboard face.
But this is meant to be
a pleasant note, because,
yes, for your birthday
I wish you happy for a change,
nothing between your ears

but a cube of perfect afternoon,
no memories at all
of good Leon using up
your youth, or of the sons
that gave you
that scar up your belly like a road,
no memories even of the boy
whose youth you twisted in your hands
like the dishtowel
that swallowed all your pain,
the child who offered you his love
in exchange for the treasure
of your tears, and you so willing
to accept the trade!
But you could surprise us by being happy
sometimes, that blue
at the center of your brain
that would hold a wasp to the light
and see it pretty.
You were pretty then,
had back from us a moment
the sacrifice of beauty
we could never repay.
And I wonder again,
will you forgive me in the end
for having scrambled out of you
and walked away,
for having left you like an empty house,
for having used you like a gate,
and not looked back?
Because of course I do—
look back, I mean,
and of course you are always there
striking a pose,

now arms (hairless as nectarines)
outstretched to a song, now shoulders
hunched over swells of asthma
or paranoias
that flew out of your eyes like bats.
Dear Tulia, if you are grown tired
then what am I
who carry you on my back?
who live you with every mile I walk?
who am the love that you regret?
Dear Tulia, when you forgive me,
will I have forgiven you yet?

The Tree My Mother Saved

The tree my mother saved by ruthlessly
cutting back the flowing, overextended limbs,
Venus de Milo of our front garden, still
impressive in its abbreviated gestures,
outlived her by two years only.
Sawing it down, we found it gutted

by blind borers and carpenter ants,
a miracle of a minor sort it had withstood
the storm of summer. Now, piece by piece,
it feeds the fire grudgingly, rotten as it is,
still too full of sap to do the flames a favor,
smoke draping off each log in heavy veils

torn by the repeated pop of sparks.
"Cut there, there," I remember her ordering
the men who clambered the branches
like ten-year-olds trying to please,
"More, more, a little more"—
waving her arms in the middle of the garden.

Lesson

The grapes peeled and cut in half, seeded, twenty
of them on a plate, how long did it take her to
prepare that treat because I would not eat them any
other way, translucent gold-green cupolas, "Do

you know about the sun, *mamá,* do you know
it stands still and it's the earth goes round,"
and she looks at me and shakes her head "No,
just check out the window you can see it go down,"

all that Saturday I went around her and she
went around me, "it looks that way *mamá* but
don't you see," until finally she stopped and she
looked hard and said, "You learn, you keep it up,

not like me, don't waste your life," and she stared
out the window, and I began to feel scared.

Frieze

The woman lying on her side,
unquestionably a woman despite
the scalped, grey cranium
and the gargoyle face distended
by postoperative distress,
is my mother teetering on the edge—

the woman with blood on her brain
and not expected to recover
the proper use of her name,
the songs that stitched
our old good days to the late bad ones,
the bulldog mind that would not
forgive nor be forgiven,

the woman who always joked of
mis quince primaveras
(the fifteen springs of her soul's age)
is twisted on her side, blanket slipped to the floor,
and they show white and bare as marble,
bare as a girl's running, the legs

of this woman still with the double
stillness of things meant to move,
one arm pinned under her, the other flung back
as the intern tries to set things straight
all round her, the solicitous tubes,
the tray of wobbly medicines by the bed,
the clipboard charting the slide of her pain—

while she, the woman, small barrel of chest
and belly robed by a single sheet
flowing over her like a breath,

more daring than any dancer, more finely
turned, more abandoned, more debonair,
has paused a moment in the lightness of her pose,
and frozen there.

Costa Rican Medicine

They offer herbs of all sorts in the open
market, some in great barrels and some
in little boxes, gold or rust or deep
brown powders, leaves green and fat or
withered into feathers, no illness goes
unmentioned, no sorrow unacknowledged
by the women and old men picking through
remedies in the dusty sun, explaining
the power of orchids, snails, black moss,
and always in a whisper to my anxious
infatuated aunt: just spice a sandwich
with this spread, hold it under your arm
for one whole day and then give it to him,
he will be on his knees before the morning.

And in the patio at the back of the house
my mother tears the cellophane off a box,
usually mustard yellow but this time
little-boy blue, piles up a small mound
on a tin ashtray and strikes match after
match until the powder sparks, unfurls
a sharp plume that she waves into her
mouth with a great wheezing, gulping
the air like some creature beached,
while always right behind her I rub
her heaving back, muscled and curved
and rounded for my practiced slaps, eight
years old, trembling, and afraid to breathe.

Twenty years later in Berkeley at the movies,
the incensed air pressed tight around my face
musty, hot, sweeping into the nostrils
in a deep kind of way, opening a hurt
I did not know was there—the smell of pot,

what did it have to do with the small
wrought iron table where my mother sat
blue with the asthma of her imagination,
how funny to think she was getting high,
I was so afraid in my small shoes, how I
rubbed and patted this woman that for me
was dear and dying and who was hardy as
a bull, drawing in the dark powers, snorting,
huffing, ready to charge.

First Communion

The vaults, the robes,
the hovering elevation of
the host, the brand
of sunlight on the back
of the small priest's hand,
the angels with their frozen
wings at the high windows,
all recollect a rosary
of abandoned prayers—
again a boy at the command of grace
I kneel, and breathe

deep as if I'd never left,
the incense afloat
in Alajuela's pink stone church,
that dim, vast place
where my brothers and I told
and retold the hail
of silver beads in our hands,
while on the other side
of the great door (*and now I
see him there for the first time,
feel him where he waited
knowing we soon must come*)
our father, tall and ruddy
and godless as a cowboy,
paced in the raw sun, his mind
dark with English
and with our futures,

while we, thoughtless as never
again, fiercely pure
and apart from him
who would not be saved,
closed our eyes

to take on our tongue
the extraordinary bread,
and our fingers fanned apart
symmetrically upon our hearts,
lending them the splendor
of pale wings.

Timex

Two weeks before his death at fifty and
two weeks after his birthday at the beach
my father gave me his watch, snapped it off
his large freckled wrist and handed it over

without ceremony, which was like him,
but young as I was I felt the warm weight
of the gift, he was just sitting on the bed
and said I want you to have this, no other word

of explanation, shoulders hunched in the brown
bathrobe as always falling open, chestful
of grey hair, swell of belly, hand extended
like an ape's palm down holding the silver-

banded numberless face, almost impossible
to read, especially in the bedroom shadow.

Fender Bender

My father relaxed his foot on the pedal and tapped
the car ahead, no mark on the bumper but the woman
jumped out in a concerned huddle of scarf and coat,
pointed to the unmarked chrome with one hand
and held the other against the back of her neck,
my father was a lawyer and shook his head,
I had no idea what the game was that afternoon

and never knew how much he had to pay to get on
with his life, the few months that were left of it,
but there was no doubt about one thing, his foot
had slipped, the mistake was made and it was
made by him for a change, the afternoon was
windy and cold and the food was in the backseat
and for some reason I was looking at his foot

when it slipped off and let life blunder in,
he even said shit and jumped out and I watched him
out the window, saw his mouth move slowly
as if taking little bites of cold and wind,
but nothing he said mattered that afternoon,
because the woman just kept touching her fender,
back and forth, she rubbed it, back and forth.

Mate

I beat Bobby Fischer, he was playing sixty
people at the same time and I was fourteen
and he was almost twenty, this was before
he pulled out the metal fillings in his molars

so the communists could not control his brain
or maybe it was the Jews, he went from board
to board quickly handsome and serious his
fingers long and strong, a Bishop's Gambit I

declined and dug in hard, he piled his rooks
around my cornered king, I pushed a pawn
and he let it go too far, his sacrifice fell just
one move short, he grinned and signed my sheet,

this was in the old days, his teeth looked strong,
not bad my father said on the way home.

Learning English

What is the meaning of this word, Father,
this small one in the middle of the page?
Do I have to look it up in the dictionary?
Can't you this once just tell me
so we can both remain where we are
together in the light Mozart brings
from the beige console, you on the sofa
with your pipe lit and your eyes shut,
me reading on the rug, stuck at a word
so simple it will never be said?

First Movement

Mozart's Violin Concerto No. 4 in D
began with a flourish up and down my spine,
fifteen years old and never held before
by bright strings spilling over my father's head,

pipe in hand, eyes smoky black, jowled
appreciator of the things of man, ex-commie
turned cabby turned lawyer at the end,
how could he sit so still with that tug in

the air, I fell to the green rug with my fist
against my chest, I couldn't help grinning
around the hurt, a funny kind of halo spun
my head, I still had to live in Maryland but

outside that room all Saturday morning shivered,
a great gold crystal just about to burst.

Witness

Alajuela, 1954

Nobody starves in Costa Rica.

In the park you can hear the mangos fall,
banana trees festoon the avenues,
guavas are in season among the poor.

It's always been that way.

But my Aunt Aída is never happy.
Red nails digging into my wrist,
every two minutes she stops

to complain to strangers who grin and trot by
chased by her last thoughts
on the government she hates like a husband.

The bastards, the bastards,
even the sidewalks are falling apart,
she hisses to the passing cars,

to the stray dogs sniffing at her skirts,
and, as a last resort, to me,
her portable audience of one,

witness to how careless people are,
how insensitive, how very blind—
adangle from her skinny brown arm,

just another of her hundred bracelets.

Aunt Aída Born Again

The God of the Last Days spirited her virgin heart
off like a dove against His thundering chest—
how He had her squeezing her fists, bitter as lemons,
into the great hollow of her chapter and verse!

What could have possessed her, what could she
be looking for in those hard lips and harder eyes
which scowled Heaven at her from a faded poster,
I wondered, a wide-eyed boy who never realized

she was more cracked than her porcelain teacups,
this woman whose slippers went crazy after roaches,
whose grey robe hid the ancient glory of her closets
and who winked and grinned when any man
    approached her,

what secret flaps flung open inside her,
what wild honey flowed sweet and free in
prayer from the hive of her ribs, I wondered, when
peeking through a crack in the night wall between us

I saw her knees dig into the rug by her bed
and the gold light gallop into her upturned face.

Claudia and Love

Her Jamaican words,
half English prayer
half Spanish curse,
chased the flies
from the kitchen
and the cat
from the fish.
The scar on her neck
crawled around like a snake
or a raised piece of lace.
She was narrow and long
as the cry of a hawk,
and between her breasts hung
the tooth of a man.
Why did she wear it?
Against the curse of love.
Whose tooth was it?
A liar and a thief's.
She loved a man, she said,
because his eyes were strange
one looking straight
at the way life was,
the other at a slant
to stare the devil in the face.
She loved him, she said,
because his fingers were fat,
softer than Jesus
on her aching back.
Now he lived in her heart
like the cold in a rock.
He left me, child,
but his smile stayed home.
She grinned at the tooth
between her finger and thumb.

The Strange Maid

Unseen, excited, we tracked Chiflis to a spot
where pavement stuttered, broke into a field
we'd never noticed, watched her disappear
behind a pickup rusting on its side, smeared

with mud, a wide sheet of metal propped
against one end. Later we snuck back to explore
the truck bed that served her for a hut, found
a towel my mother had been asking about,

some brown bottles half-filled, and over on
one side, a large can she used as a commode.
Forty years ago this was, and this morning,
her shape a few steps behind me at the end

of nightmare, for the first time I took in
the world beyond pity we'd trespassed into,
laughing like monkeys at the size of the turd
in the can, the biggest any of us had ever seen,

while back at the house wild-eyed Chiflis,
herself maybe all of sixteen, swept the hallways,
wiped the floors with vinegar, and stretched
the ironed cotton sheets over our dreams.

Doña Telela's Poem

Poets must love silence, they spend their lives
building it houses. . . . I remember where Doña
Telela lived, the shaft-dark hallway inward,
the strange daughter in the shadow of a door,

the sun where the old lady sat at the center
of the house. She liked my soft hoarse voice
and her mustache tickled, a smell of hay and
flowers especially around her neck and smooth

scarf, two yellow birds in a white cage each
on its tiny trapeze, she on her wheelchair and
I on her lap playing with a string. The inner
place was open to the sky and sometimes when

it rained it splashed near without touching
us where we sat, watching, not saying a word.

Flashback

The sun dusting the window and the dying
sounds of a guitar get crossed in the blades of a fan
to blow over me a breeze forty years old,
a memory like a hollow in the yellow heat
where wasps swarming on a mango pit
spoke of pleasure in the endless morning,
and Grandfather, always darker than I am now,
pulled his bright Panama down to his eyebrows
like layered cloud above the storm—
Alajuela, white and black with sun, now returns
the pressure of his fingers on my hand,
the look both ways on the edge of the street
that goes off into the blue of the mountains.

Why bother to cross? Why not stay put for a while,
making sure nothing is about to happen,
careful glance suspended in the yellow heat?
Grandmother's picking berries in the backyard,
she's safe there with the tiny ants at her feet,
a dragonfly poised on the patio wall.
No, there's no need to hurry today because
I am visiting, because in a house nearby
a guitar is singing, and it's not noon yet.
Over there's a valley where the buildings end,
and a lake so distant it might be a tear,
and right on the corner where we have stopped,
the English lady's sweetshop, full of light.

But we know we can't stay, can we, held here
in the hug of the yellow heat, two hearts
striped by the gold strings of a guitar?
Don't bother saying so anymore, don't bother
playing grown-up, we know we're not allowed
where the English lady keeps her trays of ice cream,
each cube stuck with a single toothpick—

Come away fast, boy, since you can't linger
under the stuttering halo of her ceiling fan,
since even she knows how to say *adios*
and Grandfather is already clearing his throat
to call out your name for the last time.

A Visit Back

A musty stillness hangs over the squat brick
and cracked cement of the massage parlor
where once stood a house that held my childhood
to the earth. A grinning Geisha beckons from
the single window and inside, in the pastel rooms,
no one's left to remember a small goat lived here once,
stayed for a week before the grown-ups made it go away.

They were impatient with things. Dogs, cats, parakeets,
and maids from Guanacaste and Limón, all came and
      went
where the goat went, a deep place adults knew about
and liked to use. Marujita, my friend, you were
      banished
there as well, exiled out of reach, and it's for
your sake I return after thirty years to this place
where we exchanged the vows of eight-year-olds.

In the locked bathroom at the end of the long hall,
we spread towels on the jade-green tile and lay down
for a kiss. There is no word but love for innocence
like ours, but we were watched and Father was told,
and the wind rose in a rage, and you were gone.
For weeks I did not know I would not see you again;
my tears, too much postponed, then never came.

Now, ashamed for having held them so long, I look up
from the sidewalk to the shadow of a woman at the
      window.
I imagine her holding her pink kimono against her chest,
looking down at me and wondering when my courage
      would
bring me to her bed. Marujita, we were Adam and Eve
here once, in this Oriental Paradiso where now others
come wanting what we had, whispering in the jade-green

shadows, the window over the sink allowing the windy
afternoon, the piece of purple heaven. If anything is
left of our kiss in that memorious darkness lingering,
may it soften their delights, lighten their hearts,
the way it did ours when we lay together holding hands,
our giggles subsiding in our chests like sheets between
gusts of wind, ready to wave in a great swell again.

White Time

White time held up to a candle, translucence of
    belonging,
the way to tie your shoes is make two rabbit ears and cross
them like this then fold one under the other and pull them
tight like this and then give me a kiss on the cheek
    already

lined and filmed with tiny hairs catching the window
    fluorescent
with possibility and ponies and coconut Popsicles and
Alajuela houses trembling in the sun, you take the paper
and fold it twice like this and then you use it carefully

to make yourself clean like this and then you wash your
hands and there you are, the bare light bulb, the rough
    little
towel, the hands holding your face one on each cheek
and the kiss and someone whistling outside the window,

Uncle Enrique dropping in for lunch with his pale hands,
the fingers pulling apart the bread, the bottle of milk
on the table, so very close to the edge . . .

Hoy . . .

Nude

The moment after he snapped it I rubbed
my eyes and saw I'd been set up, how did
he get me to step out dumb blind naked
at noon and halfway down the stairs
that led to the garden before I realized

he was crouching behind the screened
window, new Brownie in hand, giggling and
shooting, I was eight he was eleven
and had turned on me, mother gave me
his best shirts before the sleeves really

were too short, it was already pretty
obvious I was going to be taller—forty
years later he pulls off his dark glasses:
"No kidding, is that old shot still around?"
letting his arm drape around my shoulders.

Six Years Dead

This morning my mother woke up swinging,
one to the belly, one to the head, take that
you piece of lint, you bathtub ring,
you sweaty shrug, you stooped, grey, fat

unresponsive thing, my mother this morning
woke up with roller blades and red hard hat,
with spurs and eyebrows and gold pinkie ring,
where do you think you're going, what? what? what

do you think you're doing, who do you think
you are, my mother woke up and spat
the world into the room in one long string
smack in the face, and up in bed I sat

muttering, you might as well go back,
mamacita, it's too late trying to make up.

Birthday Poem

Tulita, I saw two men jump up and down
with their work boots on your coffin, trying
to force the concrete encasement into its place
in the ground where the sun
would never see it, and I thought watching,

mamacita, how I and you fought
like those two men to force our love into a space
too dark and small, so that it exploded
like a star in our faces, blinding us.
But today,

mother, is my birthday, yours too
in a way, and it is no small gift
that we are talking again. The tears
of a bad son and the tears of a good son
I offer you now to brighten your dark cell.

Día de los Muertos

Lime-sherbet green the T-shirt shows
two mariachi skeletons side by side, white
splash of skulls and rivulets of bone topped
by gay sombreros and held between them

at an angle that almost hurts, an egg-yolk-
yellow guitar marks the place of the heart
between the breasts that now fill the cloth
with breadth and bulk so when bra-less she moves

her coterie comes alive and almost dances,
and I say "almost" to be true to the friend
who sent this birthday gift to my wife, a man
given to telling the truth about things,

unlike me who watch her go by and think:
bonito, the bones and the bosom dancing.

Making Room

Chico takes advantage that nobody's around
and jumps up on the couch he's not allowed,
the potted gardenia drowsy above his head,
the long bay window hovering with sun,

Chico takes the leap and turns and shifts
on the creamy colored couch he's not allowed
to find a shady spot to rest his head,
to stretch his legs, to curl his tail around,

so much clutter scattered here and there,
papers, books, sweaters, it's hard to squeeze
a body in, to stretch out toes still dark
with backyard dirt to take the perfect siesta now,

pushing off in a pile down to the floor
Neruda and Rumi and *How Does a Poem Mean*.

Backyard with Dog

Nothing beats a cold October morning
watched from the deck streaked with sun
coffee in hand after soft boiled pesticide-
and-cruelty-free eggs and just on the other

side of the fence my friend John's house
I haven't talked to in years, but let's not
fall into that hole or into the what's going
to happen next hole or into the hole

of holes in the center of the garden, barely
covered with grass and pulling the galaxies
into it, let's lean out a little into the blue
pollen-gold air to catch the fat love roses

in their final blooming, and Chico doing
what he likes to do under the dogwoods.

Of Mere Being

You go from room to room because I'm there
or because you're thirsty and need a drink or
because there is a door where you can scratch
to be let out, the world that waits is the whole

backyard, full of shrubs calling for a little pee,
elegant raising of the leg while your eyes
follow the bird that hops across the lawn, and
if no one came to open the door you would

wait and then after a while you would pee on
the floor, much as you would prefer not to,
because the body has its demands and we obey
more or less nobly, more or less honorably,

we stretch out on our blue towel, we chew
the bone until it cracks, the marrow all ours then.

Tick

Chico likes to lick himself, last night Beth
found a tick on his chest, together we
tweezed it out and flushed it away, he
lay on his back satisfied to have us work

on him, it was three A.M. or something
but she was awake petting him because she
was having thoughts and her fingers felt
the hard bump where it didn't belong

and of course she had to wake me, it was
an emergency and we handled it,
both of us up now so might as well
make coffee and sit in bed talking,

watching Chico lick himself and yawn
and fall asleep, and then it was morning.

Crossroads Snap

Just where Guatemala and Honduras meet
El Salvador, they climbed the wooden lookout
and grinned, her ex-husband-to-be showed all
his teeth, his sly friend hung back in shadow

holding the transistor that sucked Handel's
Hallelujah Chorus from the air, she remembers
the place exactly every time she hears it, the late
afternoon, the exhausted horses, she brings out

the album, black pages falling to bits, opens to
the panorama faded and simple, hard to believe
how much life it holds and how much death,
the young woman not yet betrayed, squinting a grin,

proud not to be a tourist, proud to have come so far
to teach the Mayans how to take care of themselves.

Café of Mirrors

Here it is again, one of those moments
when human beings seem beautiful to me,
even their flaws touching, a mouth too large
on that woman, a bald spot on a boy

named Roberto, my perceiving renders
them tender, I know that they are not so,
but a knowledge within that knowledge
argues for them, gauzes each dot or blot

with a kind of love, and I myself am bettered
by this flare of neon from my head,
lighting the mirror so that I am flattered
into a grin, though I catch at the next table

a man just staring around, his goatee
diving off his chin into the rest of our lives.

Easter Wings

Christ redux and the MX missiles
alarm the Sunday *Times,* which rustles in my hands
vexing my lover's sleep
so that she cries out as if suddenly there hovered
a future over her dream.

It's then that, awkward, as I hold still
the paper wings, the clear image comes of a woman in
    mourning
on whose lap I perched to make out
the word *OBITUARIOS,*
blocked big like that as if for children,

and her index finger stopped
by a name she loved. Afterward, I took that page
bannered with accident
and fashioned a clumsy, delicate plane to toss
from room to room to room, all the morning.

Hanging on for Dear Life

Time was I made her feel safe,
standing by her crib to watch away flies
from her forehead, cross-eyed

and wondering, roly-poly babe
chubbing across the carpet on
quivering legs, then turning

into such a free young dancer, though
Mother gaping out the kitchen window
to spy evil behind the friendly faces

made her wander the neighborhood
afraid of her lengthening shadow.
In her dreams, friends on the doorstep

would lose hold of gravity and their
eyes would turn wildly in their heads.
I was there when she awoke, fallen away

from my own youth, a sad soul hiding,
but for her I was a proper, daily thing,
the orange juice, or the refrigerator handle,

always there to keep Mother in her circle
like a bear on a string, and to hold out
the delicate days like a Jacob's ladder

until she grew big enough to climb.
Now, after so many years, letting go at last
(the fingers opening to an offered palm)

I see how I must turn around to thank her,
how all those years I kept her safe she
kept me too, without knowing or meaning,

like a blown balloon a boy holds down
which pulls him toward the sky a little bit.

Long-Distance Call

When she grows faint my Aunt Carmen prays
to the Sacred Heart of Jesus and strikes herself
on the back with a heavy wooden spoon she
keeps on a hook for that purpose, it always

works, one, two, three thumps on the side
of the heart keeps the blood right she explains
on the phone a thousand miles away, what
could I say except just keep it up Aunt Carmen,

swing that spoon, I mean the woman is eighty
and weighs I don't know how many pounds, I
do know but I can't say it, I love her too much,
all her bigness is squeezed into a smallness,

neat hands and feet, Mona Lisa smile, and a voice
the wayward heart of Jesus can't resist.

As Good As It Gets

Manuel thinks his cocoa tastes sort of gross,
he licks the whipped cream off the top, takes
a bite of his cookie and wrinkles his nose,
he's tasted worse but it's no great shakes

which is too bad, I say, and lean down to blow
on my Sumatra which is much too hot, we
wanted Ping-Pong but the place was closed,
so we sit at the metal table and complain as if we

had nothing better to do, which we don't,
and there is bird song in the air or in my ear,
I can't tell for sure anymore, and Manuel wants
a Coke but we're a nickel short for the machine,

he shrugs his shoulders and grins. We're doing OK
outside the Harris Teeter, Sunday, March, today.

Y siempre . . .

Peregrine

You call to me—
            dumb,
from the stone peak,
with love I come.
My talons graze
your yellow hair,
my feathers stiffly
brush your cheek.
Your wrist is bare
and golden,
            you wear
no glove for me.

"Ricordati di me dio dell'amore"

—Sandro Penna

Where am I bound that I can't move
this windy March morning, this cold
bright opening? My heart too big
in my chest, ready to lurch out of

the nest, my fingers crooked from wanting,
few leaves yet in the stark trees.
How am I bound that I can't move
the way of humans walking to work,

but stand outside my front door staring,
saying these words to the ground and wind?:
Stay with me, world, I am not ready yet—
there is a bit of sky still in my lungs,

a bit of sea left in my eyes. Let me move
lightly into the spring, O god of love.

"Purity of Heart Is to Will One Thing"

When Kierkegaard opined on "Purity,"
how did he feel it, fancy it, some one
hundred fifty years ago? A soul-thing
more light than shape, a fact so clear it is
undogged by its own shadow? At the heart
of the heart, a whirlpool of the will?

Could be. But with our divided brains, who'll
mold from modern mind a seamless purity
to match the perfect hope he took to heart?
Now Truth's a brooding Cain at best, one
who knows exactly where his other is,
the way a shadow knows the shadowed thing.

Søren squeezes up his soul into one thing,
choosing, against all reason, God—that will-
o'-the-wisp philosophy today is
dumb about. Even in physics purity
has been split so many times that Oneness
seems as infinite a regress as the heart.

Today is Valentine's, and candy hearts
offer love their complex choices, something
for every tongue, but for me only the one
embarrassing question: What do I will?
I mean, with all of me, with that purity
Kierkegaard dreamed was where God is?

The answer is simple, after all. Nothing is
more multiple and various than my heart,
if that's where wanting is. And Purity
will serve for a nun's name, or plaything
for the mind to toss and tease at will
as clever monks once did three gods in One.

Yet I do love, and loving, choose but one.
A humble unity, but there it is.
It matters more than life or art. Who will
deny, being honest, the primacy of the heart,
that takes the simple light from one loved thing
to cover all with its promiscuous purity?

What I Mean

—for Bruce, Lyn, Tom, Vince

So many words when what I mean is only
I have forgotten the ancient places in my soul.
Will they know me, these places, when I return?
Will they receive the child climbing broken walls

into the garden? A strange boy, something
of the Jew, the Costa Rican, the Spanish, something
of the Indian eyes that saw the Irazú volcano
burst alive, and the river Marañón

mix the violent cocktail of different bloods.
I am a little bit afraid of what I mean.
What I mean is only I have forgotten
the ancient places in my soul. Are they still

there waiting? Must I go there after all?
Hush, my heart, hear what you are saying:
They are there, yes, or you would not fear them;
and you would not fear them if you did not have to go.

The Parting

A man says good-bye to his son and shuts the door
but stands unseen by the window, looking out.
The wet night crowds the house. His heart is sore
and hangs inside him like a moon of doubt.

It was not his turn to go, and so he stays.
He was as hard as a man can be with his own self.
He stands and watches, wondering. The ways
from him into the world are all through hell.

The boy outside the door wipes off his face
and stares like a newborn into the dark.
Someday, without knowing it, he will return to this
    place.
The night is a highway. He does not look back.

Watercolor of a Spanish Wall

Outside the frame the sun beats on the world
artfully remaindered, a dog and a five-year-old
struggling over a bit of trash, a priest pulling
pigtails in the shadow of Thursday afternoon,

and continents away, fire and metal in free fall
over Kandahar. Where should an easel stand
before these scenes, before dry winds that raise
dust into the wash of innocent color running

down a wall? Maybe right here, right now,
where light surprises the eye and the heart
in shapes that matter beyond meaning,
when meanings would take away all place

to stand, to hold life for a moment to a level
where things as they are are all they need to be.

In a Country That No Longer Exists

"¡Oh noche que guiaste . . . !"

In a country that no longer exists
where cinnamon crackled in the air
and red song cut through the emerald
shadows, I was taken by the hand
to the dark pool where I left

my heart; and my name was silence,
and my fear lived in that silence,
until I heard the night calling
from the waters. I took off my clothes,
the wet warmth licked my ankles,

my groin, the hair on my chest
floated in the sway of the slime,
and I sank in the blossom of the water
from the old darkness that I was
to the new darkness that I am.

Latino

Let the lamps display their blatant logic
and let the noise of their opinion be heard!
Shadows of my *abuelo* and *abuelita* will still
wing intricate designs inside my skin, dark

tattoos you must dive in to read, or trace
with the Braille of arterial blood.
Braided together by mother and by father,
fric and frac from the twist of my hair

to the peppermint swirl of my barber pole,
bilingual as light and dark, more mixed
than a martini, more split than an infinitive,
I am here, I am there, I have arrived,

that's me at the front door,
that's me at the back.

Latino Born on the Brooklyn Bridge

Seven pounds three ounces of brown clay delivered
by a blue cop cursing at the height of gridlock!
What will you wish for this boy dubbed Ariel
oh world weary with parting and arriving,

what fate for a spirit fallen on this concrete rainbow,
what pot of gold with his initials on it?
I have a few notions of my own, reading his story,
a few hopes against hope to wing his feet:

May this be the last time a policeman nabs him;
may he not live as he was born, up in the air,
neither here nor there in an unheld country;
may the hour of his life not be rushed.

And moved by the name they've given him,
I have one wish I am surprised to harbor,
the hope that he will be my representative,
a speaker of poetry and not ashamed of it,

who will manage to say what I have never said
about falling to earth only to rise again.

Green Mango Collage

Sharp slices with lime juice and salt,
puckery tears popping in our eyes,
dragonflies and gold toads and coral
in the snaky fields, white-limbed Zulema
a statue in the shadows of her room
turning alive to scold us away but laughing,
her thrown shoe, meant to miss,

still is flying toward us—David, duck!
duck Alan! duck Anita not yet born
into the ever-green weather, Grandfather
at his solitaire whistling a fado,
Aída in the kitchen poking the pressure cooker
with a long broom, it's going to pop!
it's going to pop! but it never will

because she left her husband on the third day
and because the neighbor brought a chicken
with its neck twisted on its shoulder
and the long dinner was rich with scandal,
the scent of green fruit, the rice
with almost no hard grains in it,
the coins of plantain glowing on the plate.

Bubble

Turrialba, 1953

Noon heat hunkers fragrant, loud.
Lilies are budding on the lake.
Calf-high grass quivers.

He has wanted this moment to exist:
the insect flares blue on a prickly branch,
opening and closing, the size of his hands.

His heart pumps a bubble over the world:
it holds.

After Another Death

"Nuestras vidas son los ríos . . ."

Night begins black tree shapes against grey
blue sky ruled by power lines and inside
this room the weak-tea light of the overhead
lamp and my will to put down words feeling
the concave keys resist and give against
the slightest pressure, no reason can make
sense of my desire to pattern this hour with
meaning shareable and memorable, my
fingers on my wrist find the small bone
protruding, the heartbeat of small hairs
each discernible but mingling in a rough cloud
toward the elbow, the gnawing sound of
Chico working his six-dollar bone, one
end already worn away, he and I going

at it together, my fingers on the keys, his
teeth on the bone, wearing away the hour
toward some infinity, Beth on the road
to Mebane, my uncle on the way to hell,
my aunt haunted by new freedoms in every
room of the house, Johnny alone in Albuquerque
Alan alone in Boston Juanito alone in Greensboro
and I am alone with the clean sound and feel
of keys yielding to my pressure, why not why
not I could go on and on but take a breath
listen to it escape, the sound beginning at
the back of the throat sweeping the inside
of the ears, rubbing the top of teeth on
its way into the sea of air, our lives

are rivers they are not rivers they are rivers
that go to the sea that is our death but
that is not where I am going now, the heat
has just kicked on, chess exists in the den,

Shakespeare exists on the shelf, dear ones
populate the earth, Marujita maybe still alive
walks her dog down some Quito street,
Flora maybe still alive hangs a load of laundry
out to dry, remembers me waving good-bye
half asleep in my rabbit pajamas in San José
back when grandfather played solitaire in
the kitchen not seeing how dark it was getting
until finally he got tired of shuffling and just
let his hands hold each other for a while.

Before We Knew

The day the light broke
began transparent and poised
as the hover of a wave
our dreams held back.
Just before the moment came,
everyone was awake and washed,
the fact of breakfast glittered,
the allergic cats lingered in bed,
and Father had still not sneezed.
Why was it, just then,
we were all so happy?
In the kitchen's ample air
long-eyed angels licked their wings,
and it was not going to rain after all,
and the square of sun on the table
wasn't cut by a single fly.
Yes, the morning the light broke
began frail and whole
as the halo tilted on the Virgin's head,
as round and tinted
as the tear of a saint.
It might have gone on forever,
it might have lasted the day,
but someone got careless, that's all—
someone got careless,
and that was when the bats came
and sucked the milk from the air,
that was when Mother found the mirror
and was frozen there,
touching a wrinkle by her lip,
and the neighbor-lady got pregnant
and left without a word,
and across the patio's checkered floors
black bishops gobbled up the pawns.
No, there was not a grain of corn

left in the rosaries
the day the light broke,
not a tooth in the maid's head,
not a laugh in the oldest brother—
only each of us alone remembering
what a clarity held us
just before the cracking and the splash,
what a keen edge just before the end
of the beforeness, what a transparent wing
trembling over that simple morning
when for once in each of our lives
we all woke up happy.

Mark Smith-Soto was born in his father's hometown, Washington, D.C., and raised in his mother's native country, Costa Rica. A professor of Spanish in the Department of Romance Languages at the University of North Carolina at Greensboro, he makes his home in that city with his wife, Beth, and their dog, Chico.

Photo by Bob Cavin, courtesy of the UNCG News Service.